WAR AND CONFLICT IN THE MIDDLE EAST™

AMERICA'S WAR IN AFGHANISTAN

JAMES W. FISCUS

 THE ROSEN PUBLISHING GROUP, INC., NEW YORK

For Chris Bunch, with whom I spent hours discussing Afghanistan and Middle East politics. Those conversations helped shape this book.

Published in 2004 by The Rosen Publishing Group, Inc.
29 East 21st Street, New York, NY 10010

Library of Congress Cataloging-in-Publication Data

Fiscus, James W.
America's war in Afghanistan / by James W. Fiscus. — 1st ed.
    p. cm. — (War and conflict in the Middle East)
Includes bibliographical references and index.
Summary: Discusses the war between the United States and Afghanistan in the aftermath of the 2001 terrorist attacks on New York and Washington, D.C., providing some historical context for the rise of the Taliban and Al Qaeda.
ISBN 0-8239-4552-9 (library binding)
1. Afghanistan—History—2001– —Juvenile literature. 2. War on Terrorism, 2001– —Juvenile literature. 3. Qaida (Organization)—Juvenile literature. 4. Taliban—Juvenile literature. [1. Afghanistan—History—2001– 2. War on Terrorism, 2001– 3. Qaida (Organization) 4. Taliban.] I. Title. II. Series.
DS371.4.F57 2003
958.104'6—dc22\

                                                          2003014337

Manufactured in the United States of America

CONTENTS

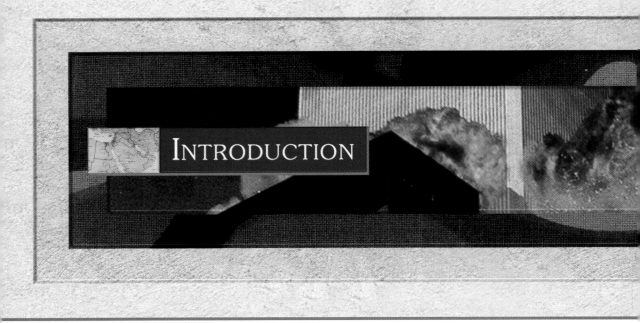

INTRODUCTION

The world is a dangerous place. War destroys lives somewhere in the world every day. Tribe against tribe. Clan against clan. Nation against nation. Few days in human history have been free of war. A million and a half Afghans died during the Soviet invasion (1979) and the civil war between mujahideen, or holy warriors, that followed the defeat of the Soviets (1989). Millions more Afghans were wounded or fled the country. As Afghanistan bled, most Americans lived in a cocoon of safety. That cocoon was shattered on September 11, 2001. On that day, hijacked jetliners crashed into the World Trade Center in New York City, the Pentagon near Washington, D.C., and a farm field in Pennsylvania. Three thousand people died in the attacks.

The attacks of September 11 were quickly tied to a radical Islamic group, Al Qaeda. Al Qaeda was based in Afghanistan. The fundamentalist Islam rulers in Afghanistan—the Taliban—had been allies of Al Qaeda for years. The

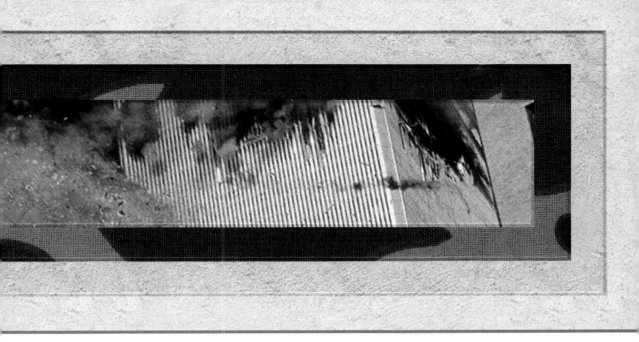

United States demanded that the Taliban surrender Al Qaeda's leaders. The Taliban demanded proof of Al Qaeda's role in the September 11 attacks and refused. The American government quickly decided that war in Afghanistan was its only option.

CHAPTER 1

BACKGROUND FOR WAR

mericans first noticed Afghanistan after the Soviet Union invaded the country in 1979. American interest, however, was limited to cheering for the Afghan mujahideen as they fought America's Cold War enemy. When the Soviet army withdrew from the country, American interest died. America ignored Afghanistan until September 11 forced its attention back to the country.

Geography, Trade, and History

High, brutally steep mountains slash from northeastern Afghanistan across the center of the country like the fingers of a giant hand. The mountains form the Hindu Kush range that divides Afghanistan into northern and southern regions. High deserts and plains ring the mountains to the north, west, and south. Even on the plains of Afghanistan, winters are cold and the summers hot. The deserts of western Afghanistan are some of the harshest on Earth. The plains of Afghanistan have been conquered many times. Sometimes, the conquerors stayed. Often, the conquerors only paused before moving on to attack an enemy empire. The people living in the mountains of Afghanistan have never been completely conquered.

Afghanistan is a southwest Asian nation landlocked between Pakistan, Iran, and Turkmenistan. The country's ethnically diverse population has witnessed some of the most brutal wars in history.

In addition to being a bridge crossed by invading armies, Afghanistan was a highway for the trade routes of the ancient and medieval world. Nearly 3,500 years ago, the Egyptians used lapis lazuli from Afghanistan to decorate the golden funeral mask of Egypt's boy king, Tutankhamen. Later trade routes led through Afghanistan linking the Middle East and Europe with India and China. Caravans of thousands of camels carried silk and other goods along the 5,000 miles (8,0346 km) of the Silk Road. Today, Afghanistan sits across a new kind of trade route. Oil and natural gas from the former Soviet republics of Central Asia may someday flow through pipelines crossing Afghanistan.

Islam and "Militant" Islam in Afghanistan

Understanding Islam is important to understanding the political and military factions in Afghanistan. The prophet Muhammad founded Islam in the seventh century. The two major divisions of Islam are the Sunni and the Shia. Shia means "party" in Arabic, and the original Shia-Sunni split was caused by a political dispute over leadership of the Islamic world in the eighth century. Today, about 85 percent of the Islamic world is Sunni. There are several sects of Shiism, depending upon which of the historic caliphs or imams (religious leaders) they follow. Americans are most familiar with the so-called Twelver Shiites of Iran. (The Twelvers follow the twelfth imam.) Today, about 15 percent of all Muslims are Shia. The largest group of Shiites in Afghanistan are the Hazaras of the central mountains. Many

Ethnic Politics in Afghanistan

The population of Afghanistan reflects the invaders who have come and gone over the centuries. Nearly all of Afghanistan's ethnic groups also live in neighboring countries. The largest group, the Pashtuns, live in southern Afghanistan and northern Pakistan. The Pashtuns make up about 40 percent of the Afghan population. Other major groups include Tajiks (25.3 percent), Hazaras (18 percent), Uzbeks (6.3 percent), and Turkomans (2.5 percent). (See map, page 10.) The percentages are estimates for 1996.

Each of the groups is divided into tribes. While ethnic groups have fought each other, tribes within the larger groups have also fought tribal civil wars. Even when the central rulers of Afghanistan have controlled the county, they have done so by forming alliances with tribal leaders.

Two main Pashtun divisions are important. The Durrani Pashtuns live mainly in the western portion of Pashtun territory, generally from Kandahar to Herat. The Ghilzai Pashtuns live more in the east, generally from Kandahar to Kabul. The Turkic ethnic groups (peoples speaking various languages related to Turkish) live mainly in the north. While some Persian-speaking groups live in the south, most are in the north and west.

The Hazaras are related to the Mongolians and live in the rugged Hindu Kush Mountains at the center of the country. In addition to being different ethnically and in language from the Indo-European Pashtuns and the Turkic peoples, the Hazaras are Shiites rather than Sunnis.

The Northern Alliance, which helped American forces in Afghanistan, is largely made up of ethnic rivals of the Pashtuns. The Taliban are mainly Pashtuns.

other Shiites also live in western Afghanistan, near Iran. The western city of Herat is increasingly a Shiite center.

Terms such as "fundamentalist" and "conservative" are applied to religious groups that claim they want to follow the actual text of their holy books. In the case of Islam, the holy book is the Koran. Within both Sunnism and Shiism, there are groups that are modern and groups that are fundamentalist. As with all religions in the world, local traditions and customs blend with Islam to give a local flavor to the religion.

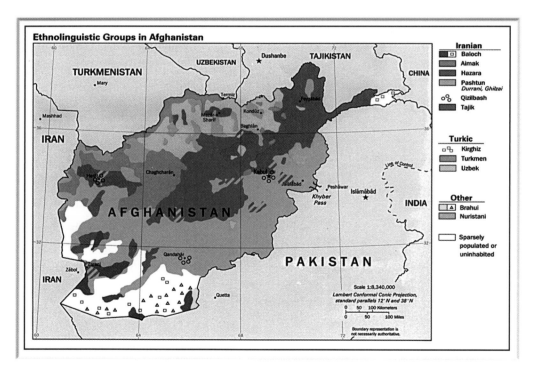

Four major ethnic groups populate Afghanistan: Pashtuns (40 percent); Tajiks (25.3 percent); Hazaras (18 percent); and Uzbeks (6.3 percent). There are also other minor ethnic groups (Aimaks, Turkomans, Buloch, others) (10.4 percent).

There are four major sects, or schools of law, in Sunni Islam. While the analogy is not fully accurate, you can think of the schools of law as being different denominations. (Think of the differences between Protestants and Catholics.) Eighty percent of Afghans have traditionally followed the most liberal Sunni school of law, the Hanafi.

Pakistani journalist Ahmed Rashid writes in his book *Taliban* that this moderate form of Islam worked best for Afghanistan. Most decisions were made by the tribes and in the villages, not in the capital, Kabul. Islam was a central part of Afghan life at all levels and helped unify the many ethnic groups in the country. Traditionally, Rashid writes, "Islam in Afghanistan has been immensely tolerant—to other Muslim sects, other religions and modern lifestyles. Afghan mullahs [religious leaders] were never known to push Islam down people's throats and sectarianism was not a political issue until recently." Much of this changed with the Soviet invasion and the civil war that followed the defeat of the Soviets. The Taliban would blend tribal law and conservative Islam, turning Afghanistan into the most conservative and oppressive Islamic state on earth.

CHAPTER 2

WAR, RELIGION, AND TERROR

In 1973, the king of Afghanistan, Zahir Shah, was overthrown by his cousin Muhammad Daoud. A Soviet-backed coup (government takeover) tossed Daoud from power in 1978. The new pro-Soviet government was weak, however. In December 1979, the Soviet Red Army invaded. Fifty thousand troops soon controlled the main cities and highways. (Soviet strength in Afghanistan would eventually near 120,000 troops.)

The Soviet invasion united the great majority of Afghans in an overriding cause—driving the Soviets out. But under that cause, all the divisions of the country remained. Most of the different groups were also fighting to protect Islam. The Afghan fighters quickly adapted the hit-and-run tactics of guerrilla warfare. They were called mujahideen, or "soldiers for God."

Supporting the Mujahideen

At the time of the Soviet invasion of Afghanistan, a military government ruled neighboring Pakistan. This government created an Islamic state, ruled by Islamic law (the sharia). Sharia law is based on the Koran and on Islamic traditions. Pakistani leaders feared that Soviet rule in Afghanistan would endanger Pakistan itself. Trade with Afghanistan was also

Soviet troops scan the highlands for the Islamic guerrillas they are at war with in this photo taken in April 1998.

important to the Pakistani economy. Pakistan wanted to control events in Afghanistan for religious, political, and economic reasons.

Pakistan's military intelligence organization, called Inter-Services Intelligence (ISI), began sending guns and money to the mujahideen. Throughout the war against the Soviets and during the civil war that followed, the ISI was the main pipeline used to help the mujahideen. Religious conservatives dominated the ISI. As a result, moderates and fighters who did not want to create an Islamic state in Afghanistan received little support from the ISI.

Americans think of the Shia as being the most militant branch of Islam because of the Islamic state in Iran. The Sunni can be just as militant. Saudi Arabians follow a sect of Islam founded in the late 1700s called Unitarianism or Wahhabism. The power of the Saudi royal house is completely tied to the Wahhabis. The sect is one of the strictest, most fundamentalist forms of Islam. The Saudis spend a great deal of money to support fundamentalist forms of Sunni Islam in many countries. They did so in Afghanistan.

Pakistan began sending weapons to the mujahideen while Saudi Arabia and other oil-rich Arab states sent money. Both nations concentrated their support on the most militant and religiously fundamentalist of the mujahideen. The United States's Central Intelligence Agency (CIA) became more and more involved in training and supplying the mujahideen as the war continued. The CIA channeled most of its aid through Pakistan's ISI. Thus,

American aid went to the fundamentalist groups and not to secular (nonreligious) nationalists.

The war quickly fell into a stalemate. The Soviets held the cities and major bases. The Afghans held the mountains and rural parts of the country and attacked Soviet convoys and bases. The war was bloody on both sides. Nearly 3 million refugees fled to Pakistan. Once in Pakistan, the refugees lived in giant camps. The Saudis and

In this photo, Afghan mujahideen raise their rifles in triumph while posing over the wreckage of a downed Soviet helicopter. This image was taken on May 13, 1979, during the Soviet invasion of Afghanistan.

others funded religious schools (madrassas), where the refugees learned the most militant forms of Islam.

Even before the strain of the Afghan war, the Soviet Union was in poor economic shape. The Afghan war cost more than the Soviet economy could afford. Since shortly after the invasion, America had been sending modest amounts of aid to the mujahideen. In 1985, the CIA began to ship Stinger antiaircraft missiles to the mujahideen. Stingers soon

Afghan guerrillas pose jubilantly on a captured Soviet armored personnel carrier in this photo taken in April 1980. The tide would turn many times during a war that would become a stalemate between the two sides, until the Soviets left in frustration later that decade.

began knocking Soviet helicopters and planes out of the sky. The price of holding Afghanistan suddenly went up—just as the Soviet Union was growing tired of the war. By early 1989, the last regular Soviet troops left Afghanistan.

The many mujahideen factions immediately began fighting each other. Pashtun leaders were disorganized and unable to take advantage of the Soviet withdrawal. In April 1992, well-trained Tajik and Uzbek forces captured Kabul. The Tajiks were commanded by Ahmed Shah Massoud. Massoud was the best military commander among the mujahideen. The Uzbeks were led by General Rashid Dostum. For the first time in 300 years, Pashtuns were not in control of the capital. Pakistan continued to back Pashtun warlords as the civil war kicked into high gear.

Blowback and the Rise of Militant Islam

"Blowback" is a term used by the CIA and other intelligence services to describe when a military, political, or intelligence operation leads to results that are against the interests of the people carrying out the operation. Blowback struck both the Soviets and the nations that sent aid to the mujahideen. Before the Soviet invasion, there was little sign of Islam in the Soviet Central Asian republics (which are now the nations of Turkmenistan, Uzbekistan, Tajikistan, Kyrgyzstan, and Kazakhstan).

The first Soviet army into Afghanistan had many units from Central Asia. Even though the Central Asian troops were quickly replaced with troops from European Russia, the damage had been done. The returning soldiers brought the ideas of militant Islam home with them from Afghanistan. Seeking in part to break the hold of traditional Islam on Afghanistan, the Soviets instead helped those ideas spread into their own territory. The Soviets are still fighting militant Islamic rebels in Chechnya.

The Pakistanis and Saudis supported the most militant of the mujahideen. Pakistan now faces thousands of trained

In this photo taken on May 16, 1988, Afghani onlookers wave flags as Soviet troops ride out of the capital city of Kabul during the Soviet withdrawal from Afghanistan.

Islamic fighters on its own territory. The largely Pashtun Northwest Frontier Province of Pakistan adopted the most conservative form of Islamic law in early 2003.

During the war against the Soviets, an estimated 35,000 foreign Muslims flocked to Afghanistan to fight with the mujahideen. As many of them were supported by the Saudis and came from Arab countries, they were called Afghan Arabs. During the years of war against the Soviets, the Afghan Arabs learned how to fight a guerrilla war and became more and more militant. The return of thousands of these Arab Afghans to Saudi Arabia and the rest of the Middle East continues to cause problems for both moderate and conservative Arab nations. The Saudis, in particular, face trouble at home as a result of the return of trained fighters. Several bombing attacks in the country are blamed on veterans of Afghanistan.

The massive aid the CIA and others sent into Afghanistan did help defeat the Soviets. Pakistani journalist Ahmed Rashid says the mujahideen received about $10 billion in aid from the United States and the other nations. (The Soviets spent $45 billion trying to defeat the mujahideen.) Nearly all of the American money and guns ended up in the hands of the most radical mujahideen leaders. In the end, American aid helped build the Taliban and Al Qaeda into threats to America. Some observers suggest that the United States and the Western world would have been safer today if we had let the Soviets control Afghanistan.

Civil War and the Rise of the Taliban

The religious and social beliefs of the Taliban grew from Pashtun tribal customs and ideas of Islamic militants. These militants fought the modernization of Afghanistan. The brutality of the Taliban grew from twenty years of war that destroyed the country. More than 1.5 million Afghans died and millions more were wounded and maimed. More than 3 million fled to refugee camps in Pakistan.

In many ways, the mujahideen civil war was worse than the war against the Soviets. The Soviets had held the cities and kept them safe while they destroyed the villages and the countryside. Many people fled to the safety of the cities. As the civil war spread, the safety of the cities was destroyed. The civil war destroyed Afghanistan's cities as warlords rained rockets on civilian and military targets alike.

Ahmed Rashid reports that Mullah Omar and the top leadership of the Taliban had nearly all been wounded in the long fighting. The majority of their soldiers, however, were too young to have fought the Soviets and came from the refugee camps in Pakistan. Most were trained in Islamic schools in Pakistan, the madrassas. The madrassas are mainly funded by the Saudis and conservative Pakistanis.

After Kabul fell to Tajik and Uzbek troops, the Pashtun warlord Gulbuddin Hikmetyar attacked the city. Hikmetyar proved to be one of the most vicious of the mujahideen commanders. Over the next several years, Hikmetyar fired thousands of rockets into the city. He

In this picture taken on November 8, 1996, a Taliban fighter armed with a plastic whip stops a man on a bicycle to force him to attend Friday prayers. Resentment of the Taliban had grown since its takeover of Kabul weeks earlier, due to the group's extreme religious zeal.

could not take Kabul, but he could destroy it. Hikmetyar was supplied by Pakistan.

Other cities suffered nearly as much as did Kabul. Making the entire situation worse was the destruction of traditional agriculture during the Soviet war. The Soviets had bombed and bulldozed orchards and farmland. The irrigation system needed to keep the orchards alive was destroyed. Millions of land mines left by both the Soviets and the mujahideen blanketed grazing land. The farmers turned to growing opium poppies to survive.

The Taliban stepped into the chaos. Mullah Omar was running a small madrassa near Kandahar. Villagers complained to Omar about attacks from local thugs. Omar gave rifles to some of his students and began to enforce order, usually by capturing the suspected criminals and executing them publicly. Success led to more success, and the Taliban grew. Students from the Pakistani madrassas joined the movement.

Pakistan has a large Pashtun population, and 20 percent of its army is Pashtun. Pakistan and the ISI were increasingly desperate to find Pashtun leaders who could capture Kabul. By 1993, it was clear that Hikmetyar had failed. Pakistan began to watch the new movement. In October 1994, the Taliban captured a large arms dump. A month later, it captured Kandahar. Pakistan's powerful trucking mafias soon paid bribes to the Taliban and drove convoys through its territory.

At least 25,000 non-Afghans who had fought against the Soviets returned to Afghanistan over the next few years to fight with the Taliban. Other fighters from conservative madrassas in

Central Asia and Pakistan flocked to join the Taliban. (Perhaps 60,000 came from Pakistan alone.) Fighters also arrived from Egypt, Sudan, Jordan, Palestine, Iraq, Yemen, Algeria, Nigeria, Morocco, Tanzania, the Philippines, China, Britain, and even the United States. The Taliban used the foreigners to fight its enemies and to terrorize the Afghan population.

The Taliban Takes Hold of the Country

Over the next two years, the Taliban fought to take Kabul. The Taliban often called on the madrassas to send more young men to help in the fight. Each call was answered by thousands of young men who had been raised in the desolate refugee camps. The Taliban's manpower and the aid from Pakistan and Saudi Arabia finally won the day. In September 1996, the Taliban captured Kabul. (The next year, Massoud and other opponents of the Taliban formed the United Front for the Liberation of Afghanistan, generally called the Northern Alliance.)

The Taliban immediately clamped a vise of Islamic fundamentalism on Kabul. Opponents were tortured and executed. Women were brutally driven from work and from public life. Women had made up a quarter of the workers in the civil service and nearly all of the elementary school teachers. Under the Taliban, if women failed to clothe themselves from head to foot, they faced torture and death. The Taliban established the strictest Islamic government on the planet. The Taliban's ideology owed as much to traditional Pashtun tribal law as it did to the Koran and Islam, however.

The Taliban's rules against allowing women to work or receive an education forced some women to the lowest rungs of Afghan society. Even women who had no male relatives to support them were not allowed to work.

Ahmed Rashid points out that most of the Taliban's young soldiers had no knowledge of the complexity of Afghan history. They did not understand the traditional balancing of ethnic groups and interests. Most had also grown up in the camps and did not understand life in the villages and cities of Afghanistan. They had never seen Afghan women—mothers, aunts, grandmothers, and sisters—participating in daily life and running homes. In the madrassas, they had studied the Koran and Islam. But they had learned little of the world outside the camps. Thus, they took easily to the extremism and brutality of the Taliban.

The civil war continued. In every city the Taliban conquered, it took total control. Even local allies were killed or driven out. The Taliban killed thousands of Shia Hazaras. Herat rose against the Taliban, and the citizens killed hundreds of Taliban soldiers. The Taliban soon retook the city. By early 2000, the Taliban controlled most of the country. Only Ahmed Shah Massoud and a few others held out in their territories in the north. Most of the money and guns for the northern forces now came from Iran, Russia, and the Central Asian republics. Each of these countries feared the Taliban and its form of Islam. Pakistan and Saudi Arabia still supported the Taliban while the United States and Europe largely ignored the country.

Al Qaeda and the Taliban

Osama bin Laden had founded Al Qaeda during the war against the Soviets. He left Afghanistan after the Soviet

Osama bin Laden and Al Qaeda

Osama bin Laden and his Al Qaeda organization are responsible for the terrorist attacks on the World Trade Center and the Pentagon on September 11, 2001. Bin Laden is, above all, fighting to end American influence in the Middle East and to replace the al-Saud dynasty in Saudi Arabia.

Bin Laden was born in about 1957 to a wealthy and powerful family in Saudi Arabia. His father, Mohammed Awad bin Laden, moved to Saudi Arabia from the Hadramout during the 1930s. (The Hadramout is the southern coast of Arabia from the Omani border to the city of Aden. It is now part of Yemen.) Mohammed Awad built the largest construction company in Saudi Arabia. The family became extremely wealthy.

Osama bin Laden was educated in Saudi schools and universities but has never traveled outside of the Middle East. He knows little of the outside world. His family was devout, and bin Laden moved more and more toward a militant form of Islam. Immediately after the Soviet invasion of Afghanistan, bin Laden began collecting money to support the mujahideen. He is believed to have been in Afghanistan as early as 1982. Two years later, he used his money and connections to set up a guesthouse in Peshawar, Pakistan, to help Arabs fighting the Soviets. In 1986, he set up his own guerrilla and terrorist training camps for the Arabs flocking to Afghanistan. Two years later, he founded Al Qaeda.

"Al Qaeda" means "the base" in Arabic. Bin Laden used Al Qaeda to aid the Arab Afghans and keep track of their activity. He had strong support from both the Pakistani and Saudi intelligence services. Money also came from wealthy Saudis and part of bin Laden's own fortune.

During the war against the Soviets, bin Laden appears to have received training from American CIA operatives. After the Soviet war, bin Laden returned to Saudi Arabia. Reports indicate that he had not yet turned against the Saudi government. Iraq's invasion of

Kuwait in 1991 changed bin Laden. He offered to bring the Afghan Arabs to Saudi Arabia to help defeat Saddam Hussein. Then America sent troops to Saudi Arabia to help drive Hussein out of Kuwait. But the Americans were also infidels to bin Laden. For him, they were invaders in Islam's holiest land.

Bin Laden turned against the Saudi royal family. He recruited several thousand men to help fight the American "attack" on the country and sent them to his training camps in Afghanistan. At about this time, bin Laden's family rejected him and his attacks on the Saudi royal family. The Saudi government revoked his citizenship in 1996.

Osama bin Laden creates the overall political and military goals for Al Qaeda rather than being involved in detailed planning for terrorist attacks. Bin Laden stresses the importance of guerrilla warfare rather than direct confrontation. In other words, attack where your enemy is weakest, not against your enemy's strong points. Long preparation with careful planning is normal for Al Qaeda operations. The preparation can take three or four years and perhaps longer.

Before the destruction of the World Trade Center and the attack on the Pentagon on September 11, 2001, bin Laden and Al Qaeda carried out a number of other major attacks. In 1993, Al Qaeda operatives set off a truck bomb in the basement of the World Trade Center. Al Qaeda is believed to be responsible for the 1996 bombing of a U.S. barracks in Saudi Arabia that killed nineteen Americans. The organization bombed American embassies in Kenya and Tanzania in 1998. And in October 2000, Al Qaeda agents bombed the destroyer USS *Cole* while it was in the Yemeni port of Aden.

At the time this book is being written, no one can be sure if bin Laden lies dead in a collapsed cave in Afghanistan or if he is still alive and planning further attacks. It is widely believed that he is still alive. In either case, Al Qaeda appears to now be a loose coalition of individuals and groups operating worldwide. Cutting off its head will not necessarily destroy Al Qaeda.

defeat but returned in May 1996. Later that year, he issued his first call for jihad (holy war) against the Americans he believed were occupying Saudi Arabia. Al Qaeda would use terrorist attacks to fight bin Laden's war.

Bin Laden soon became friends with Mullah Omar. He then moved to the Taliban capital of Kandahar. The Taliban handed over several training camps to bin Laden and Al Qaeda. Bin Laden issued repeated calls for war against America and the West. After the Al Qaeda bombings of the

This photo, taken on April 7, 1998, shows the damage done to the Co-operative Bank House in Nairobi, Kenya, after a bombing that day. The bombings of American embassies in Africa in 1998 were largely attributed to Al Qaeda terrorists.

U.S. embassies in Africa in 1998, bin Laden's reputation grew. Less than two weeks after the bombings, the United States sent some seventy cruise missiles crashing into Al Qaeda camps. The camps were largely empty, however. Fewer than fifty Al Qaeda members were killed.

Once in Kandahar, bin Laden moved closer to the Taliban. Ahmed Rashid points out that before bin Laden's influence, the Taliban was not especially anti-American. After America's cruise missile attack on Afghanistan, the Taliban's words turned sharply against America. It began using bin Laden's language in attacking the Saudis and other pro-Western Islamic regimes.

In the late summer of 2001, bin Laden repaid the Taliban's hospitality by killing its greatest foe. Two Al Qaeda agents pretended to be Algerian reporters sent to interview Ahmed Shah Massoud. On September 10, Al Qaeda assassins exploded a bomb that killed Massoud.

The next day, Al Qaeda struck directly at the United States.

CHAPTER 3

THE AMERICAN WAR IN AFGHANISTAN

American intelligence agencies quickly tied the September 11 attacks to Al Qaeda and Osama bin Laden. The United States demanded that the Taliban surrender bin Laden. The Taliban said it would not turn over a "guest" and demanded proof that Al Qaeda had been involved. Pakistan's ISI tried and failed to convince Mullah Omar to give up bin Laden.

Mullah Omar and the Taliban had little understanding of the world outside Afghanistan. They had seen the Soviets defeated by the mujahideen and did not understand the reach of American power. The United States had 15,000 men stationed in the Middle East and the Indian Ocean. The carrier *Carl Vinson* and its battle group circled in the Persian Gulf while the carrier *Enterprise* waited in the Arabian Sea. Eight days after September 11, the nuclear carrier *Theodore Roosevelt* and its battle group sailed from Norfolk, Virginia. The carrier *Kitty Hawk* left Japan, packed with helicopters rather than jets.

The United States Strikes Back

America's greatest problem was finding targets in Afghanistan. The Soviets had destroyed the countryside. The mujahideen civil war had destroyed the cities. The United States could bring destructive power unrivaled

The USS *Enterprise*, an aircraft carrier stationed in the Indian Ocean, is shown in this image from October 9, 2001, during the U.S. invasion of Afghanistan.

in history against the Taliban. But there was little in Afghanistan worth attacking. One official who had served in President Bill Clinton's administration was reported by the *New York Times* as saying that when they had studied attacking Afghanistan, the sense was they "were going to have to bomb them up to the Stone Age." President George W. Bush also seemed to understand the problem, saying, "What's the sense of sending $2 million missiles to hit a $10 tent?"

The United States readied its special operations and quick response forces. The army's Special Forces Command and sections of the 10th Mountain Division mobilized. The commander of U.S. forces in the attack on Afghanistan was General Tommy Franks, who headed Central Command (CENTCOM). Franks would later command U.S. forces during the 2003 invasion of Iraq.

Pakistan was trapped in a problem of its own making. Pakistani aid had been critical in helping the Taliban take over Afghanistan. Now, Pakistani president Pervez Musharraf realized that the Taliban was out of control and endangered Pakistan. Musharraf was also outraged by the September 11 attacks. He promised full support of the United States in fighting Al Qaeda and the Taliban.

The United States talked with the council of the North Atlantic Treaty Organization (NATO) and presented its evidence against Al Qaeda. NATO nations agreed to help. On October 6, 2001, President Bush issued a final warning to the Taliban. The next day, America and Great Britain attacked, calling the war in Afghanistan Operation Enduring Freedom.

Some forty land-based and carrier-based bombers struck. Tomahawk cruise missiles were launched from British and American ships in the Arabian Sea. B-1 strategic bombers flew from the Indian Ocean island of Diego Garcia. Meanwhile, B-2 stealth bombers flew all the way from Missouri. Navy F-14 and F-18 fighter bombers flew from the carriers. Taliban bases and command centers were smashed. The small air force the Taliban had inherited from the Soviets

This October 10, 2001, photo shows bombs falling from a U.S. B-1B Lancer over an undisclosed location in Afghanistan. The B-1B is one of several long-range bombers that took part in the bombing campaign of that autumn.

was largely destroyed on the ground. The attacks devastated the Taliban's few Soviet-era SA2 and SA3 antiaircraft missile batteries. As attacks continued, AC-130 Spectre gunships raked the ground with their Gatling guns and cannons.

Not all went well for NATO forces, though. The Taliban moved out of its bases and into the countryside. American planes quickly ran out of targets. Despite claims that "smart bombs" always hit their targets, they often missed. Sometimes the error was one of faulty intelligence. The bombs hit a target, but it was the wrong target. Sometimes the technology failed, and the bombs and missiles missed their targets. In one major incident, American bombs struck the United Nations compound in Kabul. In another, a 2,000-pound (907-kilogram) bomb hit a family home in Kabul.

Special Operations Begin

By mid-September, a twelve-man Army Special Forces (Green Berets) A-team began working on the ground with Northern Alliance forces. By early November, at least four teams were in the country. As John Carney and Benjamin Schemmer, authors of *No Room for Error: The Covert Operations of America's Special Tactics Units from Iran to Afghanistan*, point out, the special operations troops faced rugged conditions. Winter on the Afghan plains was freezing. Mountain ranges averaged 9,000 feet (2,743 meters) in elevation. Most of the time, the Special Forces wore Afghan clothes, not their high-tech, cold-weather gear. Carney and Schemmer say that over the next few months, 190 special operations men would be sent to Afghanistan. The force involved 70 percent of all "special tactics personnel based in the U.S." with additional units arriving from Europe.

Special Forces were joined by paramedics and by combat controllers who directed U.S. bombing attacks. Special tactics teams from the air force surveyed twenty-one Afghan airfields. Four of them were in Pakistan, according to Carney and Schemmer. Air force teams managed air traffic control at some fifteen airfields used by U.S. forces. They directed

Providing cover for other members of his strike force, a U.S. Navy SEAL is shown here on February 1, 2002, well into the Afghan war. He is one of many special operations forces that did most of America's fighting during the Afghan war.

more than 8,000 sorties (a single flight by a single airplane) from these fields.

Special operations also staged independent raids. The first major commando raid struck on October 19, 2001. Helicopters from the carrier *Kitty Hawk* dropped Green Beret troops on one of the Taliban's headquarters. While they failed to capture Mullah Omar, they blew up bunkers and equipment. Five Special Forces men were wounded by their own explosives.

At the same time, Army Rangers parachuted onto an air base south of Kandahar. The attack was basically an armed reconnaissance (exploration). While the Rangers were pulled out safely by helicopters, nearly two dozen had been injured during their parachute drop. One of the Rangers' helicopters crashed in Pakistan, killing two of the crew. Apparently discouraged by the lack of real success and the injuries, the U.S. command ordered no more raids for some time.

Air Support for the Northern Alliance

The Taliban faced the Northern Alliance north of Kabul. American aircraft began bombing Taliban positions in late October. Before American attacks on the front lines, Taliban troops had felt safer there than in their bases. The Northern Alliance had fought for years without air support. Now it was happy for the help. It joined the attack with rockets and artillery.

Soon, however, cracks showed in the attacks. Northern Alliance soldiers told the *New York Times* that the Taliban quickly got used to the American attacks. Taliban soldiers were making fun of the American bombs over their radios. U.S. planes had long flights to the combat area and arrived every so often in pairs. The Taliban would hunker down for a few minutes, then emerge to fight after the jets left. Stephen Tanner, in his book *Afghanistan: A Military History from Alexander the Great to the Fall of the Taliban,* quotes one Northern Alliance soldier who told the *New York Times*, "When Soviet troops invaded Afghanistan, sixty airplanes would strike one place, while one hundred tanks attacked it. If the [American] attack continues like this, the Taliban morale will be very high." Other reports said that after a day and night of bombing, only ten bombs had hit the Taliban.

The great problem for American air power was that the Taliban fought from fortified bunkers and trenches. The United States used 5,000-pound (2,268-kg) laser-guided bombs and 2,000-pound (907-kg) bombs guided by lasers or from satellites to attack Taliban bunkers. The air force also flew repeated missions with the B-52 strategic bomber. The huge plane can carry 70,000 pounds (31,752 kg) of weapons. It can deliver traditional bombs, cruise missiles, and the new "smart bombs" and bunker busters. B-52 raids would appear to destroy a half-mile of Taliban defenses. But once the raid was over, the Taliban would crawl from caves and trenches and continue fighting. Many of the bombs were simply missing their targets. In response to its inability to hit its targets in the first attacks, the United States sent observers to the front lines. U.S. Army,

Air Force, and Navy forward controllers arrived to direct attacks and tell pilots where to drop their bombs.

Both tactical aircraft and artillery are most effective when there are spotters, or forward controllers, on the ground near the targets. The forward controllers direct the attack and correct for errors. With artillery, they may give orders to fire left or right, for example. With laser-directed bombs, the controller may actually highlight a target with a laser

Looking on at plumes of smoke in the distance rising from U.S. bombings near the village of Rabat, about 30 miles from Kabul, a U.S.-allied Afghan Northern Alliance fighter is shown in this photo from November 12, 2001.

beam. Controllers can also send the exact position of the target they want hit, using the global positioning system (GPS). The plane and its bomb or missile home in on the laser or are directed to the GPS coordinates.

American bombing became much more effective. The combat controllers directed more than 600 close air support attacks that delivered more than 4,500 bombs. Carney and Schemmer report that one air force team directed air attacks from horseback while riding at full gallop to save Rashid Dostum from being overrun by the Taliban.

The Need for Ground Troops

No matter how devastating an air attack may be, infantry is needed to take and hold ground. As the war progressed, the United States seemed unwilling to use its regular army and marine units on the ground against the Taliban. American planners decided to use local anti-Taliban troops supported by U.S. special operations units to do the hard fighting. The United States wanted to fight the ground war in Afghanistan using proxies (substitutes).

By November, the war began to shift into higher gear on the ground. Ismail Kahn, a Tajik mujahideen leader, returned to the Herat area and rallied his former fighters. The Uzbek leader, Abdul Rashid Dostum, reorganized his forces in the north as well. In the central Hindu Kush, Hazaras organized and attacked the Taliban.

Dostum and another Northern Alliance general attacked the city of Mazar-i-Sharif. They quickly captured the airport. Many Taliban troops followed Afghan custom and switched sides. Most of the others surrendered or fled. Members of the Taliban who escaped to the east were boxed in by Ismail Kahn.

Other Northern Alliance forces attacked the northeastern cities of Kunduz and Taliqan. A Taliban commander with at least a thousand largely Pashtun troops at Taliqan switched sides. The city fell on November 11 without fighting.

Members of special operations forces, such as Air Force Special Tactics operator master sergeant Bart Decker, often had to adopt the ways of their Northern Alliance allies—such as riding on horseback rather than motorized vehicles—in order to make it through the harsh Afghan terrain.

Special operations troops attacked as well. The British Special Air Service (SAS), probably the best special operations force in the world, was operating in Afghanistan. In one widely reported engagement, a sixty-man SAS Sabre team attacked a tunnel held by about the same number of Taliban members. Four SAS men were wounded. Some eighteen Taliban died, and more than forty were captured.

Herat fell to Ismail Kahn on November 12. The Northern Alliance swept south toward Kabul. Taliban members fled for their homes or defected. Mullah Omar abandoned Kabul, ordering the Taliban to "Take to the mountains." U.S. air power shattered columns of Taliban troops retreating to the south.

Taking Kabul and Battling in the North

The United States and Pakistan did not want the northern troops to enter Kabul. Both feared that if the capital fell to Uzbeks and Tajiks, the Pashtuns would rally to support the Taliban. That would restart the civil war. But Kabul lay open. On November 13, Northern Alliance troops entered the city. The Taliban's rule had been harsh and bloody in Kabul. Most residents greeted the Northern Alliance troops as liberators.

As Kabul fell, the Taliban abandoned the southern city of Jalalabad. A mujahideen leader who had been based in the Pakistani city of Peshawar claimed Jalalabad. Rumors circulated that one of the bloodiest of the Pashtun warlords, Gulbuddin Hikmetyar, would return and take his traditional territory south of Kabul. Soon, he did return. Ismail Kahn held Herat.

Dostum controlled Mazar-i-Sharif. As Tanner says, "Aside from the lamented Massoud, all of the major players of the Soviet war and the mujahideen civil war were reassuming their positions." Taking quick advantage of the recent victories, British Royal Marines and American Special Forces were flown into Bagram air base north of Kabul. Bagram became a major base for U.S. operations in Afghanistan.

Most of the Taliban had now been driven from northern Afghanistan. Kunduz, however, was held by Arab Afghans and other foreign volunteers. They were hated by the local Afghans and could not simply change sides. The foreigners had no option but to fight. The Northern Alliance surrounded the holdouts and asked for their surrender. The Afghan Taliban wanted to surrender. The foreign Taliban, however, fired on the Northern Alliance forces. The siege went on.

The Northern Alliance reported that Pakistani cargo planes flew into Kunduz to rescue Pakistani fighters. Other Taliban members fled into the countryside. Near the end of November, about 700 Pashtun Taliban surrendered to the Northern Alliance. They left their battle lines smiling and waving. They were greeted with cheers. Meanwhile, nearly 1,000 non-Afghans fought on.

The Qala Jangi Revolt

Kunduz fell on November 26. The foreign fighters were taken prisoner by Dostum's troops. Four hundred of the prisoners were moved to the ancient fortress of Qala Jangi near Mazar-i-Sharif. The rest were waiting to be trucked to the fortress when the prisoners already at Qala Jangi revolted.

Apparently, two American CIA agents had been questioning the prisoners when one of the Taliban grabbed a guard's weapon. Other prisoners joined the revolt. CIA agent Johnny Michael Span was killed as the prisoners seized the huge fortress.

Qala Jangi had been a weapons dump, and the prisoners were soon well armed. U.S. and British air controllers directed air strikes against the fortress while Dostum's Uzbeks waited. Dostum's men attacked after the bombardment and drove the Taliban underground. Moving through the huge fortress, the Uzbeks poured oil into the basement and set it on fire. They fired rockets into other basement chambers. The last eighty Taliban were captured on December 1 after the rooms they hid in were flooded. More than 200 Taliban and forty Uzbeks died in the hard fighting. One of the Taliban recaptured was an American, John Walker Lindh.

Taliban Defeat and Aftermath

During November, the 15th Marine Expeditionary Unit landed south of Kandahar. Aside from special operations forces, the 2,500 marines were the first U.S. ground troops in Afghanistan.

On December 7, rival Pashtun warlords captured Kandahar. The troops commanded by the different warlords immediately began shooting at each other. The mujahideen were falling back into the civil war the Taliban had ended. Meanwhile, the fighting against the Taliban continued.

The last Taliban province surrendered on December 9. Everyone was surprised at the speed of the Taliban's fall. The failure of the Pashtuns to support the Taliban was especially shocking.

When Pakistan cut off aid to the Taliban, the Taliban was left without fresh supplies of arms and men. The Taliban had been welcomed when it ended the mujahideen civil war. But the harshness of the Taliban's rule turned people against it. Opium also appears to have been an

Life appears to return to normal in Kabul after the ousting of Taliban forces by the Northern Alliance. Here, citizens visit the city market on November 15, 2001. Residents were initially overjoyed at being free from the repressive Taliban regime.

important factor. Growing opium poppies had become the only cash crop for many poor Afghan farmers. In 2000, the Taliban banned the growing and sale of poppies. The ban turned even more Afghans against the Taliban.

Efforts to create a new Afghan political structure moved forward. In December 2001, Hamid Karzai was chosen as interim head of government by Afghan leaders in Bonn, Germany. Karzai was a Durrani, the same subgroup of the Pashtuns as the last king of Afghanistan. Karzai and other leaders began building the new government in Kabul. In June 2002, a Loya Jirga—a traditional tribal council—elected Karzai president of Afghanistan.

CHAPTER 4

HUNTING AL QAEDA

Mullah Omar, Osama bin Laden, and most of Al Qaeda's leaders remained at large. The CIA believed that bin Laden had retreated to a mountain fortress Al Qaeda had built in southeastern Afghanistan. Tora Bora sounds like a South Pacific island. In fact, it is a complex of fortified caves in extremely rugged mountains near the Pakistani border.

Afghan troops supported by a few U.S. special operations troops closed in on Tora Bora. Even in peacetime, the Pakistani army had been unable to control the tribal regions near its border. Despite this, American leaders believed Pakistan when it now said it could and would seal its border to block escape by Al Qaeda fighters. The United States also offered a reward of $25 million for bin Laden.

U.S. defense secretary Donald Rumsfeld reported that the United States would take direct action to crush the holdout forces at Tora Bora. A week later, Rumsfeld called off use of American troops. The Defense Department apparently feared the public's reaction to American casualties. The United States called on the Afghans to continue the fight on the ground.

Tora Bora fell after heavy bombing and hard fighting by the Afghans. Bin Laden was not found. After the failure at

Osama bin Laden is flanked here by his deputies Ayman Al-Zawahiri *(left)* and Muhammad Atef.

Tora Bora, the United States stopped relying on Afghan fighters as much. Instead, elite units of between 100 and 300 U.S. troops would attack with only a few local interpreters. The troops would land from helicopters or drive to a site. They would then search the village or suspected hiding place for Al Qaeda fighters. The new raids started in early January 2002. They showed growing U.S. initiative but failed to capture many Al Qaeda leaders.

One of these raids shows the complexity of Afghan politics. Late in January, the 101st Airborne attacked what it believed was a Taliban arms stockpile. Twenty-one Afghans were killed and twenty-seven captured by the paratroopers. The army soon learned that the base had not been a Taliban hideout at all. Reporters who investigated learned that the base was controlled by the Karzai government in Kabul. It was a collection point for captured weapons. The 101st released the men taken prisoner.

Stephen Tanner analyzed the mission as a case of turnabout. The 101st had acted on intelligence from an Afghan warlord. It had already staged other raids on similar information. Now, apparently, Afghan factions were feeding the United States false information so that it would attack their rivals. "While the U.S. had originally used Afghans as proxies, it now seemed that the Afghans were doing likewise with the Americans," Tanner wrote. The warlords used "units like the 101st Airborne or [called in] U.S. air strikes to resolve their local feuds."

Operation Anaconda

Early in March 2002, the United States launched Operation Anaconda. It was the largest U.S. ground attack so far in the Afghan war. The plan was for about 900 Afghan troops to attack up the Shah-i-Kot Valley. The valley was believed to be a refuge for 150 to 250 Al Qaeda fighters. Meanwhile, 1,200 U.S. troops would be lifted by helicopter to block the

U.S. troops examine the mountain ridges for signs of Al Qaeda and Taliban forces during Operation Anaconda on March 4, 2002, in Sirkanel, in eastern Afghanistan. The objective of the operation was to finish off what remained of enemy forces after major combat ended.

escape routes from the valley. They would be joined by 200 commandos from Australia, Canada, Denmark, Germany, France, and Norway.

On March 2, 2002, U.S. bombers hammered the suspected Al Qaeda refuge. The Afghan troops attacked but were stopped by heavy fire. An American adviser was killed. The Afghans retreated. Meanwhile, the U.S. troops and other commandos landed in their blocking positions. They came under massive fire from enemy machine guns, mortars, and rocket-propelled grenades (RPGs). Two days after the start of the attack, a Chinook helicopter was hit. The chopper swerved suddenly, and a navy SEAL was tossed out of the door. He was killed by Al Qaeda fighters. His rescue beacon still called for help, however, and help was sent.

A Chinook loaded with troops from the 10th Mountain Division was shot down a mile from the first attack. The downed troops were hit by enemy weapons fire. Six died and eleven were wounded. Throughout the valley, other U.S. units from the 10th and the 101st found themselves pinned down by heavy fire as well. Several dozen men were wounded. The Americans fought back with their own machine guns and mortars. Attack helicopters raked the enemy with fire. Over the next week, U.S. and French jets and American helicopters pounded the valley.

The U.S. command said it believed that at least 1,000 Al Qaeda and Taliban troops had moved into the valley from Pakistan. On March 13, General Franks of Central Command claimed more than 500 dead enemy fighters, with hundreds more wounded. By the end of the operation, the confirmed and believed dead count of the enemy rose to 800.

When American reporters reached the valley on March 13, they found only three enemy bodies. There had been a hard fight against Al Qaeda and Taliban forces, and Americans had died. But, as often happened during the Vietnam War (1964–1975), the numbers of the dead enemy had been badly overestimated. The U.S. command blamed the retreat of the Afghan troops for part of the mess. However, the Afghans were stopped, at least in part, because they had been attacked by a U.S. C-130 Spectre gunship. The Taliban and Al Qaeda fighters knew the mountains. They most likely slipped away after the first day or so of fighting.

Despite the failure to capture bin Laden, the United States took control of hundreds of prisoners in the war. Most were suspected of being hardcore Taliban or members of Al Qaeda. More than 600 were eventually moved to the U.S. naval base at Guantánamo Bay, Cuba. Others were held at U.S. bases in Afghanistan or elsewhere. The U.S. government reports that some of the prisoners have revealed important information during their time in captivity.

CHAPTER 5

LOOKING TO THE FUTURE

In Afghanistan, the United States received help from several thousand troops from Canada, Britain, Australia, and other nations. About 7,500 American troops were in Afghanistan by July 2002. The European Union had also agreed to supply a small peacekeeping force in Kabul. It was named the International Security Assistance Force. As of June 2003, U.S. Central Command reported that there were some 15,000 U.S. and allied (non-Afghan) troops in Afghanistan. Less than half of them—

some 7,000—were Americans. Bagram Air Base north of Kabul is the largest foreign base in the country. Press reports estimate that 11,500 troops are stationed at Bagram.

Meanwhile, the Bush administration was more interested in Iraq and the buildup toward the American attack in the spring of 2003. Afghanistan was put on the back burner of foreign interest. Allied troops patrolled Kabul, but neither the allies nor the Americans tried to police the countryside. Most of Afghanistan was again left to the warlords.

Still, operations to find and destroy Al Qaeda and the remainder of the Taliban continued. U.S. troops continued raiding suspected Al Qaeda and Taliban bases. Intelligence operations have led to the capture of Al Qaeda leaders. In March 2003,

A Turkish soldier of the International Security Assistance Force patrols downtown Kabul on November 5, 2002. International peacekeepers are still stationed in Afghanistan.

Khalid Sheikh Mohammed, a senior Al Qaeda commander, was captured in Pakistan. Information from Mohammed apparently led to a raid by 1,000 U.S. troops southeast of Kandahar in an unsuccessful effort to find and capture bin Laden.

Karzai Tries to Rebuild Afghanistan

Throughout late 2002 and early 2003, the Karzai government begged Western governments for promised economic aid.

U.S.-backed Afghan president Hamid Karzai is sworn in at Kabul's presidential palace on June 24, 2002. The Afghani grand council, or Loya Jirga, chose Karzai as the first leader of the newly formed government. As of the writing of this book, Kabul is one of the few stable areas in the country.

But the aid seemed to only dribble into the country. While the Kabul government has survived and may even have slowly gained strength, the warlords rule the country.

In one example of how serious the situation is, Hamid Karzai's minister of defense is a Tajik warlord, Muhammad Qasim Fahim. Fahim commands the new Afghan army that is being trained by the United States and France. But Fahim refuses to pull his Tajik troops out of Kabul. Thus, the minister of defense maintains a private, ethnic army loyal only to him. Worse yet, Russia has promised Afghanistan $100 million in military equipment. Ahmed Rashid reports that the Russian aid "will flow to Fahim's [private] army" and not to the national Afghan army.

In another example of foreign aid in Afghanistan that may undercut the Karzai government, Iran is aiding western Afghanistan. Iran has spent $15 million to build power lines from Iran to the city of Herat. Iran is selling power to the residents at a loss, according to a June 2003 report in the *Washington Post*. The paper also reports that Iran has spent $38 million building a highway from its border to the city. Iran has also promised $560 million over five years to rebuild Afghanistan. The aid includes building and maintaining schools. The *Post* reports that the Iranian form of Shiism is becoming more popular in the region.

The Comeback of the Taliban and Al Qaeda

With the continuing chaos in Afghanistan, the Taliban appears to be regrouping and making a comeback. In early

June 2003, Afghan troops killed forty Taliban hiding in a village near the Pakistani border. The Taliban had raided a regional center near the Pakistani border. The small force was resting when troops loyal to the governor of Kandahar attacked them.

Also in early June, four German soldiers who were members of the International Security Assistance Force were killed by a car bomb in Kabul. Dozens of other people were wounded. There is a strong indication that the terrorist bombing was carried out by members of Al Qaeda or the Taliban.

Ahmed Rashid reported from Lahore, Pakistan, on June 5, 2003, that Karzai's government was in desperate need of stronger security. He wrote in the *Telegraph* (London):

> Experts believe America's refusal or inability to take the lead in providing Afghans with greater security is pushing the country back to the anarchy and lawlessness that gave rise to the Taliban and allowed [Al Qaeda] to base itself there.
>
> Regrouped Taliban are rocketing, bombing or ambushing United States and Afghan government forces in the south and east where humanitarian aid and reconstruction, which has barely started, are grinding to a halt.

An Unstable "Victory"

When the United States launched Operation Enduring Freedom in Afghanistan, the Afghan people were sick of the

Taliban. They were more than ready to carry the bulk of the fighting needed to bring it down. With the fall of Mullah Omar and his thugs, Al Qaeda lost a secure base that was important to its operations. But both the Taliban and Al Qaeda survive. Al Qaeda has struck again, most recently, at the time of this writing, in Saudi Arabia.

In Afghanistan, ethnic warlords have carved up the country again. Most of the warlords are financed and supplied by one or more of the nations bordering Afghanistan. Growing and selling opium also helps pay for many of the tribal armies. Russia, Iran, and Pakistan are major players. In Pakistan, the Pashtun Northwest Frontier Province bordering Afghanistan adopted a strict form of Islamic law in early 2003. Wealthy Saudis still send money to fundamentalists in Afghanistan and Central Asia. As this is written, it appears that Afghanistan is slipping into the kind of chaos that first led to the rise of the Taliban. The United States has proclaimed victory over the Taliban. But victory is often hard to judge. It will be years before the United States knows if it has truly won or lost its war in Central Asia.

GLOSSARY

Army Rangers A unit that falls between a true elite special operations force and regular troops.

jihad The primary meaning of jihad is the internal struggle of an individual to live by the laws of the Koran. The secondary meaning of jihad is more commonly understood by non-Muslims. It is often called holy war. The external jihad is the fight to defend or expand Islam.

madrassas Islamic schools. Students study the Koran, usually by memorizing much of the book.

mujahideen Arabic for "soldiers for God." The soldiers are often called holy warriors.

Northern Alliance Formally called the United Islamic Front for the Liberation of Afghanistan (UIFLA). An alliance of non-Pashtun groups formed to fight the Taliban.

special operations Special operations troops are more highly trained than regular troops. They usually operate as small units. U.S. special operations forces include the U.S. Army's Special Forces and Delta Force, the Navy's SEALs, and units from the Marines and Air Force.

Taliban The militant, fundamentalist, Islamic group that took control of Afghanistan, ending the mujahideen civil war. Its name comes from the Arabic word *talbi*, meaning "student."

terrorism The use of violence to create fear and terror, usually used against civilians.

Organizations

Amnesty International (U.S. office)
322 Eighth Avenue
New York, NY 10001
(212) 807 8400
e-mail: admin-us@aiusa.org
Web site: http://www.amnestyusa.org

Center for Afghanistan Studies
University of Nebraska at Omaha
Omaha, NE 68182-0006
(402) 554-2376
Web site: http://www.unomaha.edu/~world/cas.html

Women's Commission for Refugee Women & Children
122 East 42nd Street
New York, NY 10168
(212) 551-3111 or (212) 551-3088
e-mail: wcrwc@womenscommission.org
Web site: http://www.womenscommission.org

Web Sites

Due to the changing nature of Internet links, the Rosen Publishing Group, Inc., has developed an online list of Web sites related to the subject of this book. This site is updated regularly. Please use this link to access the list:

http://www.rosenlinks.com/wcme/amwa

Ali, Sharifah Enayat. *Afghanistan*. New York: Marshall Cavendish, 1995.

Caldwell, John C. *Pakistan*. Broomall, PA: Chelsea House Publishers, 2000.

Carney, Col. John T., and Benjamin F. Schemmer. *No Room for Error: The Covert Operations of America's Special Tactics Units from Iran to Afghanistan*. New York: Ballantine Books, 2002.

Ewans, Martin. *Afghanistan: A Short History of Its People and Politics*. New York: HarperCollins, 2002.

Gritzner, Jeffrey A. *Afghanistan*. Broomall, PA: Chelsea House Publishers, 2002

Kazem, Halima. *Afghanistan*. Milwaukee, Wisconsin: Gareth Stevens Publishing, 2003.

Miller, Charles. *Khyber, British India's North West Frontier: The Story of an Imperial Migraine*. New York: Macmillan, 1977.

Nojumi, Neamatollah. *The Rise of the Taliban in Afghanistan*. New York: Palgrave, 2002.

Rashid, Ahmed. *Jihad: The Rise of Militant Islam in Central Asia*. New York: Penguin Books, 2002.

Rashid, Ahmed. *Taliban: Militant Islam, Oil and Fundamentalism in Central Asia*. New Haven: Yale University Press, 2001.

Tanner, Stephen. *Afghanistan: A Military History from Alexander the Great to the Fall of the Taliban*. New York: Da Capo Press, 2002.

BIBLIOGRAPHY

Aziz, Javed. "Sharia Law Adopted in Pakistani Province," *Guardian*, June 3, 2002.

British Broadcasting Company (BBC) News. "Al-Qaeda Killed German Troops." June 11, 2003.

Burke, Jason. "The New 'Great Game': Torture, Treachery and Spies—Covert War in Afghanistan: War on Terrorism: Observer Special." *Observer*. Retrieved June 6, 2003 (http://observer.guardian.co.uk).

"40 Taliban Killed in Afghan Fighting," *Telegraph* (London), June 5, 2003.

Carney, Col. John T., and Benjamin F. Schemmer. *No Room for Error: The Covert Operations of America's Special Tactics Units from Iran to Afghanistan*. New York: Ballantine Books, 2002.

Griffin, Michael. *Reaping the Whirlwind*. London: Pluto Press, 2001.

Hubbard, Mark. *Warriors of the Prophet: The Struggle for Islam*. Boulder, CO: Westview Press, 1998.

Nojumi, Neamatollah. *The Rise of the Taliban in Afghanistan*. New York: Palgrave, 2002.

Rashid, Ahmed. Various Articles from *Far Eastern Economic Review*, 2003 (http://www.feer.com).

Rashid, Ahmed. Various Articles from the *Telegraph* (London), 2003 (http://www.telegraph.co.uk).

Terzieff, Juliette. "Taliban Shadow Falls on North West Frontier," *Guardian*, June 4, 2003.

Witt, April. "As U.S. Retreats, Iran Puts Its Money into Afghan Province," *Washington Post*, June 17, 2003.

INDEX

About the Author

James W. Fiscus is a Portland, Oregon, writer and photojournalist. He has a master's degree in Middle East and Asian history and has taught military history. In addition to writing about history, he reports on medicine, science, business, and law.

Photo Credits

Cover © Reuters New Media Inc./Corbis; pp. 1, 38, 44 © AP/World Wide Photos; p. 3 © John Moore/AP/World Wide Photos; pp. 4–5 © Chao Soi Cheong/AP/World Wide Photos; pp. 6–7, 10 courtesy Perry-Castãnedia Library Map Collection/The University of Texas at Austin; pp. 12–13 © Alexander Sekretareu/AP/World Wide Photos; pp. 15, 16 © Hulton/ Archive/Getty Images; p. 18 © Patrick Robert/Corbis; p. 21 © Santiago Lyon/AP/World Wide Photos; p. 24 © Kathy Gannon/ AP/World Wide Photos; p. 28 © Khalil Senosi/AP/World Wide Photos; pp. 30–31 © Jockel Finck/AP/World Wide Photos; pp. 33, 40 © AP/World Wide Photos; pp. 35, 46–47, 49 © Corbis; pp. 52–53 © Vincent Thian/AP/World Wide Photos; p. 54 © Zhao Peng/AP/World Wide Photos.

Designer: Nelson Sá; **Editor:** Mark Beyer;
Photo Researcher: Nelson Sá.